Printed in Great Britain
by Amazon

47228184R00059

Sue J. Daniels

Trauma Therapeutic Workbook
80 key points for Working Towards
Post Traumatic Growth

Trauma Writers Publishing

Lincoln, England.

A CIP catalogue record for this title is available from the British Library.

ISBN 978-1-9160933-1-7 (Paperback)

www.traumaresourcesshop.co.uk

First Published (2019)

Trauma Writers Publishing
12 Nichol Hill
Louth
Lincolnshire
LN11 9NQ

Trauma Therapeutic Workbook

80 Key Points for Working Towards

Post Traumatic Growth

A practical therapy workbook for those affected by life threatening or vicariously traumatic events.

PTSD and associated symptoms are just one of the conditions that can occur in the aftermath.

It has been an honour to know and to work with so

many who have been affected by any type of trauma along their life's sometimes, treacherous path.

I hope that this workbook goes some way to

giving you the tools that you might find useful to get

on with the your new life, to process the traumatic information and to be free, happy and empowered in your own right.

With Love from
'The Author'

Introduction;

What actually is Trauma?

So what is trauma? Trauma is what happens when a part of the brain reacts to a life threatening or life endangering event, it is the body's fight, flight or freeze reaction kicking in – it is an acute stress response and its aim is quite simple – to keep us safe.

The Trauma Tunnel

Imagine walking towards a tunnel: the proverbial tunnel ~ you can see a very small light in the distance. Right at this point you have a choice whether to continue towards that light or not enter the tunnel at all.

That's a nice choice, a useful option. When an individual faces or witnesses a life-threatening incident they will have no choice but to go through that tunnel. For some people the light may stay the same, get bigger or go out completely, it can be as if someone has flicked a switch in their head and all clarity of mind has been put on hold as they struggle to find their way through their own level of darkness.

When a person freezes, (in order to survive) a hormone in the brain called the amygdala holds every detail of the incident and acts like a constant bodyguard keeping the victim on high alert for further attack, using a process known as 'Pattern Matching'.

The FFF (Fight, Flight, Freeze) response prepares us for action, to either fight, when faced with danger or to run away when fighting isn't an option. These days we rarely have to face tigers or situations that may endanger our lives or be in a position where the FFF response is appropriate. However this basic understanding of the FFF response is crucial to understanding the stress that many of us face when asking for help or assistance.

This is what happens in the human body when faced with a life-threatening situation:

- Adrenaline is released from the adrenal glands (situated above
- the kidneys).
- Red blood cells flood to carry oxygen – blood is diverted to wherever it is needed.

- Breathing becomes rapid to provide more energy.
- Lungs dilate to get more oxygen.
- Sweating Increases.
- Vomiting may occur.
- Bowels become loose, urination.
- Muscles tone in readiness.
- Heart beat speeds – blood pressure goes up.
- Mouth dries up – because we don't need the saliva.

All of this happens in a split second – and it is only after the incident when the body calms down, that we are able to work with the aftershock.

The famous flight or fight response to trauma is familiar to many, but few know that the 'freeze' response is the most risky of the trio, since it inhibits any reaction and leaves the victim immobile. It can lead directly to Post Traumatic Stress Disorder and/or related symptoms.

Which way will you go...?

TRAUMA comes from the Greek word meaning 'Wound'.

T	Terror –	Absolute, wordless fear
R	Rumination –	Uncontrolled thinking
A	Abreaction –	Triggered responses
U	Uncontrollable –	Thoughts and feelings
M	Mindfulness –	Taking control of your own core being
A	Awareness	

T – Write down how the terror of what happened may manifest for you...this might present in a number of different ways, such as feeling more frightened than usual?

R – Make a note of the ways that you might ruminate over what has happened.......?

A – Can you describe how you relive what has happened, this might be when you are triggered by something connected to the incident?

U – In what way/s do you think about the incident when you don't mean to?

M – Write down how you have found ways to take control of your body and mind and ways that you have yet to master.

A – Notice that being aware of everything that has happened and learning to make sense of it all, is one small step towards your recovery.

Learn to breathe slowly into your abdomen, through your nose for the count of seven.
Then breathe out of your mouth for the count of eleven.

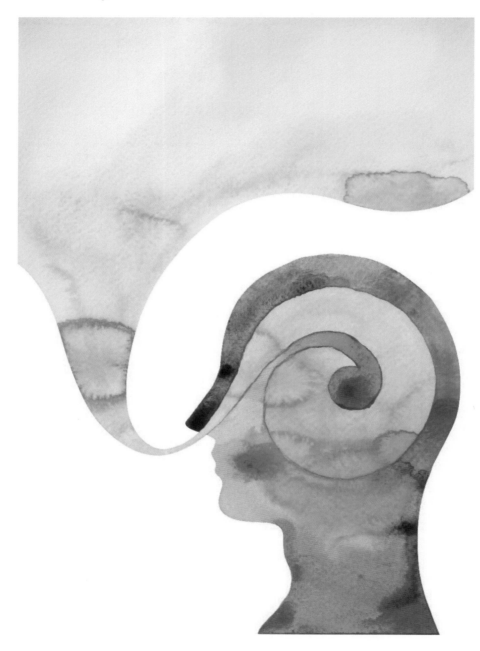

Slow down, Calm down, Don't worry,
Don't hurry, Trust the process.
Alexandra Stoddard

PTSD – Post Traumatic Stress Disorder.

Post-Traumatic Stress Disorder is a term more commonly associated with the military – its historic term being 'shell-shock'. Sadly the condition was not fully understood and often to the detriment of those suffering from it - labelled in some of the following ways:

- Absconding - Scared
- Running Away- Chicken
- Desertion
- Cowardice
- Lack of moral fibre (LMF)
- Mollycoddling
- Stress
- Burn Out

The truth is, that those suffering from a trauma often in the form of Post-Traumatic Stress Disorder are actually living in their own private hell, in their unique and all-encompassing prison.

PTSD is a reaction to being exposed to an event, which is outside the range of normal human experience. It is a normal human emotional reaction to an abnormal situation. Everyone reacts differently to different situations and it doesn't have to be a life threatening experience for someone to respond in this way. It just has to be perceived by the victim as a traumatic event. It is a psychological phenomenon. It is an emotional condition, from which it is possible to make a full and complete recovery. PTSD affects hundreds of thousands of people who have been exposed to violent events such as rape, domestic violence, child abuse, war, accidents, natural disasters, bullying, childhood sexual abuse, taken hostage, kidnap, torture and many other situations. It is normal to be affected by trauma. There is help, and it is ok to ask for help. PTSD is not rare. It is not unusual. It is not weak to have PTSD. The person experienced, witnessed, or was confronted with an event or events that involved actual or threatened death or serious injury. PTSD can develop following the experience of or witnessing a life-threatening event. Posttraumatic stress disorder is generally defined as a condition where the sufferer experiences recurring, distressing and intrusive memories and other symptoms after involvement in a traumatic event.

Psycho educational information.

Here's a story about a man called Mark Wilkinson. He was walking through a Park in Manchester, England, on his way to work one fine morning. It was April and the sun was shining. There were workers cutting the grass for the first time, ready for the spring season. In the distance, children squealed and played happily in their red gingham spring dresses before school and people ambled about the park. Some were eating and drinking breakfast from paper plates and cups as they talked and laughed together, some sat on benches reading newspapers.

Suddenly, from nowhere, a huge dog ran towards Mark and launched itself at his neck, ripping into his flesh, his body froze and he collapsed into a heap on the ground as the dog continued to rag him back and forth. Just as quickly as the dog had appeared, its' owner saw what was happening and called it, running off with it very quickly. People ran from every corner of the park to help him and an ambulance soon arrived to take him to hospital.

Within two weeks, he was feeling better, he knew he'd been very lucky to have survived the attack and was discharged from hospital with forty two stitches and two crutches. Mark had lots of practical support and recovered very well with the help of his friends and family, they never left him out or made him feel inadequate in any way. Two years later, when Mark had been married for just over a year, his wife had asked him to take their tiny daughter Poppy, out for a stroll in the buggy so that she could get some housework done. By now he lived in another town, far from Manchester. As he walked up the street he noticed the familiar smell of fresh cut grass and he started to feel a bit odd but he couldn't understand why. He thought he might be coming down with a cold.

Not wanting to go home and disturb his wife so soon, he decided to keep walking and to go and have a look at the new Italian restaurant which had just opened at the top of the street. The new restaurant had two huge open panes of glass as shop frontage, allowing for full view of the dining area, as he looked through the window, his eyes focussed on the many red gingham tablecloths, his heart raced and he started to panic, he didn't know why at this point he just felt as if he couldn't breathe. His baby daughter was asleep and blissfully unaware as he sat down on some steps, desperately trying to calm down and to gather his thoughts.

He was having a full blown panic attack, hardly able to breathe but he somehow managed to ring his wife, she came and took him home and he refused to leave the house for many weeks, which turned into months after that. Mark went to his doctor and was prescribed anti-depressants which consequently had their own side effects.

His wife left the marital home to stay at her parents as she could not cope with his panic attacks and unreasonable behaviour.

Mark was unable to go to work and subsequently, after so much time of absence, he was relieved of his duties. In just over two years he had lost everything.

~5~

Terrifying Trauma Triggers

When a person has been through the horrors of a traumatic incident and their life has been threatened, over time the brain, having taken in all of the information at each violent incident, automatically provides a technique called pattern matching, which, like a radar, reminds the person of all of the significant environmental information. Just as the smell of the fresh cut grass and gingham table cloths affected Mark.

The pattern matching acts as a reminder of the possible dangers and that the last time Mark for example, smelled freshly cut grass or saw red gingham, his life was threatened. It is a perfectly normal response and is in place to help us survive.

When a triggered moment occurs, such as the sound of shouting or fighting, it may cause your whole body to shake, your heart to pound and you may feel dizzy and disorientated. Your mouth might be dry and you experience remembered terror like a distorted film running in your head. You can become so spaced out that nothing else matters.

Triggers can occur in many areas, sometimes it can be a look, a telephone call or a colour even. It might be the same colour as a car in an accident or on an item of clothing worn by a violent perpetrator.

Smells, tastes and even visual images of similar people and/or objects, buildings that look similar or were present at the time of the traumatic event. The triggered memories can be so subtle but so overwhelming that you can feel unable to make sense of what is happening.

6

Paralysing Panic Attacks

You can suddenly hear your own heart beating and feel unable to breathe, so unfamiliar is it to you, that you actually believe you are going to die, you are in fact, abreacting. In other words, the memory is so profound that it feels like you are back at the incident to the point where adrenaline has been released from your adrenal glands (situated just above your kidneys).

Red blood cells flood to carry oxygen – blood is diverted to wherever it is needed. Your breathing has become rapid to provide you with more energy. Your lungs have dilated to give you more oxygen.

Sweating may have increased, and you are likely to feel sick, but you can't. You need the toilet badly, which is your body's way of making your body lighter for purposes of flight. Your muscles may have tightened and you are like a coiled spring. Your blood pressure may also be raised as your body reminds you of the terror and violence that you experienced previously.

All of these body responses may be happening to you in a split second, even though it might feel and seems much longer. The silence in your head is often deafening as you endure these ruminations and memories, as your brain appears to be hijacked by the terror that you have experienced and by everything else that happened to you.

7

Horrifying Hypervigilance

Jumping at every little sound, nerves on edge, constantly on high alert. The ripples of this can make not only you, but those around you, jumpy and over nervous. It is an enhanced state of awareness that primarily keeps you safe by reminding you of possible dangers that may be related to the incident. This is normal, you are normal, what happened to you is not normal.

Basically, your body is always on high alert and in preparation to fight or flight or freeze just as it did at the time of the terrifying incident.

8

Straining Sleeplessness

There is nothing worse than going to bed, ready to get some sleep and then finding yourself just lying there, hour after hour as your body remains on high alert. The effects of lack of sleep can alter the mind as it tries to make sense of the world in a fog like state.

The long term effects of sleep deprivation are real, the body need a certain amount of rest to function at its optimum level. It is when the restoration of cells and chemical balances take place.

During the sleeping state, the brain rewires in accordance with the neurons that fire together and the processing of all waking state activity is processed into the appropriate part of the brain.

Without enough sleep, the brain and body systems won't function normally and sleep deprivation can be responsible for a lower quality of life.

There are many ways to readjust your sleep pattern to its normal regulatory system, however, if you have information such as images, thoughts, memories and emotions connected to the many traumatic incidents of violence, it may just be time to seek some post trauma therapy, which will help you to process the information that is keeping you wide awake.

9

REM – Rapid Eye Movement

Every night when we go to sleep, our brain is hardwired to take us through a rapid eye movement system, ensuring that we safely file away all the information received during the day.

When a person has suffered a traumatic event, the consequential effects are often accompanied by disturbed sleep patterns.

During post trauma processing, such as EMDR, VKD or BSP the therapist will facilitate replication of the REM process whilst you are in the waking state. This is how unprocessed information can be safely put away in the memory bank where it can be safely stored and with the earlier emotional impact lessened.

Healing Your Inner YOU

If you were involved in a traumatic incident/s, your mind and body may remember what happened to you and will seek to remind you whenever it is necessary to protect you from similar incidents or further harm. This could play out in many ways such as an aversion to the place where it happened or anyone or anything that might take you back to it happening again.

It can take a huge amount of guts and courage for survivors of trauma to find a voice and speak out about what has happened and this book may help you to make a start.

EMPTY 'RAGE PAGE' EXERCISE......

Draw a picture of someone or something about the incident that has annoyed you, and rip it up into tiny pieces – dispose of as you wish and move on.....

Colouring is an old favourite when you really don't feel like talking or actively engaging with others, giving time and space to be creative with colour and to reflect and imagine using new and positive thoughts.

It's what we do after we fall,
that creates or destroys our spirit.
~ Author Unknown

~13~

Personal Reflective Journal Notes...

Your body can hold onto the traumatic incident as well as your brain.

If you decide to find professional help, it's important that you find a therapist who is trained and competent both areas of processing.

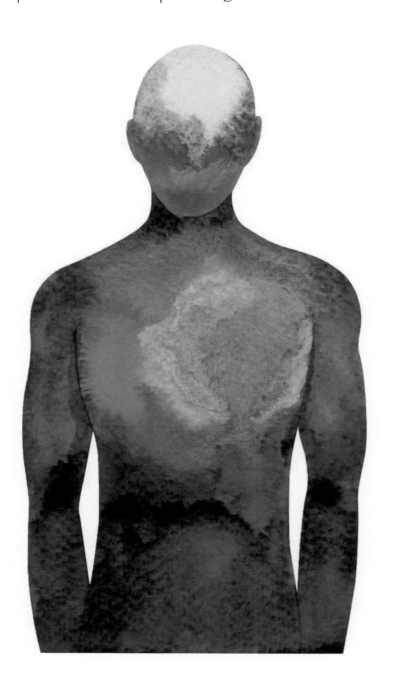

Personal Reflective Journal Notes...

Day to Day Mindfulness

Self-Safety Assurance Technique

If you happen to be laying in your bath or doing any day to day normal function, start to assure yourself of how safe you are...for example

Okay, so I am washing my dishes...

The dishes in the sink of the house that I live in......

The house that I live in that has double glazing.....

The double glazing in the house that keeps me safe....

The safety that I feel now keeps me well and happy......

The happiness I feel is because I survived......

It is not happening now.................

I am safe now...........

You can continue with this wherever you are and wherever your safety is not compromised, but each time that you do it and speak out loud, you continually empower yourself further about how safe you are now...

Out with friends

In your car

At work

On your own at home

At college

In a supermarket

In a cinema

Nutrition and Exercise....

Trying to process trauma, expends a great strain on our equilibrium and general wellbeing – not to mention the cost to family, friends and relationships. One of the best defences can only be to arm ourselves with good nutritious food. Cutting out sugary or chemically laden drinks and trying to get out for a brisk walk wherever possible can empower and strengthen.

We've made our own recipes for nutritious smoothies that will keep you motivated and energised for longer.

Our bodies respond with the hard wired fight or flight system in accordance with stress levels in the body.

Stress can play havoc with our digestion process whilst it focuses on the parasympathetic nervous system (calming it down) this can affect how food is processed as it is considered as a non-essential function for life.

A waiting period of up to thirty minutes is required for a calm environment, which, aids digestion allowing the body to break down the nutrients.

Empowering Energy Smoothie

Ingredients:

2x Big Juicy Oranges (peeled)
2x Bananas (peeled)
1x Ruby red grapefruit (peeled)
2x Carrots
Handful of Seedless Grapes
Large bio plain yoghurt – or Greek Yoghurt

Method:,

Put all ingredients through the juicer, add yoghurt and fresh bottled spring water.
Place in flask or suitable container in the fridge to chill.
Take with you to drink throughout the day.
Research the best tasty ingredients to suit your own taste and/or find the help of an established nutritionist in your area.

Find and tell someone who you trust, what has happened. Let them help and support you throughout your recovery process and beyond.

Remember that you are reacting normally to a completely abnormal situation.

~19~

Personal Reflective Journal Notes...

THE NOW YOU

Ideas to identity who you are **Now**....using taste, smell, feeling, thought and visual - all of your five senses **to create and establish the** NOW YOU.

1.   Buy a brand new fragrant shower gel or soap that you've never used before such as strawberry or zesty lemon and associate this new scent with the NOW YOU.

2.   Decide on a new colour scheme for your favourite room in your home.

3.   Purchase the softest and warmest cuddliest blanket for colder evenings in front of the TV or for when listening to music.

4.   Try a new food, associate the new taste with the NOW YOU.

5.   Eat and sleep well, nurture yourself, with good wholesome food.
      Try and get yourself back into a regular sleep pattern.
      Sleep is medicine for every cell in your body.

Sometimes it's good to research, find and purchase a new picture or wall canvas that makes you feel happy, for a favourite place in your home. Be kind to yourself, indulge yourself, in the NOW YOU.

Forgive yourself, now is not forever and you will survive this ....

Your brain has been temporarily taken over by the traumatic event/s that you have endured. The traumatic information may need to be processed intensively for the impact to lessen, which will allow your brain to clear, so that you can think clearly and begin to live again.

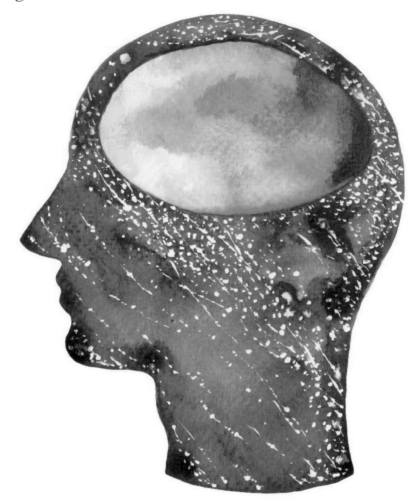

A trained therapist (there are many all over the world) will be able to work with you to facilitate the process safely and effectively.

There are wounds that never show on the body, that are deeper and more hurtful than anything that bleeds"

Laurell K. Hamilton

~23~

Personal Reflective Journal Notes...

You are not going mad – you are reacting normally to an abnormal situation...

It's always your choice to work towards post traumatic growth.....

When you take responsibility to seek healing for yourself, you accept that you are worth the time and effort involved to make positive changes in your life. This is a brave first step, the first of many, on the road to recovery.

You may begin to doubt your own memory or deny the reality and severity of the incident/s. This did happen to you and YOU DID NOT cause it to happen.

~25~

Personal Reflective Journal Notes...

When looking for a professional – take note of the following do's and don'ts – they might help you to find the right person for you.

1. Do expect to be listened to effectively, so that if the professional had to recall your story they would be able to without leaving anything out.

2. Do expect your experience to be acknowledged, understood and your recollection of events believed.

3. Make sure that you know how the professional will work with you so that you know what to expect and which aims you are working towards.

4. Don't be put under pressure to work faster than you are prepared to ~ you need to work at a pace to suit you.

5. The professional may offer you a terms and conditions or contractual agreement that will lay out the ethical boundaries under which they work, be sure to read them thoroughly so that you know what is expected of you in terms of cancellation policy etc.

6. The professional should under no circumstances, talk about their own issues, experience or life – the sessions are about YOU.

7. Ensure that the professional you are working with is fully qualified to work with trauma, it is okay to ask or search for information about them on the internet.

8. Expect to NOT be judged or told what to do next, if the professional that you have chosen does not seem able to assist you then they may know someone who can. Not every therapist is trained to work with processing interventions or trauma.

It's not weak to ask for help, it's just deciding whether or not you need professional help just to get through some of the unfinished stuff. It's completely your choice.

Learn to relax where possible, try to find extra time to invest in yourself, such as a soothing massage. You could try reflexology, walking or just simply resting, swimming, sauna or steam room.

Use whatever you need, whatever suits you to feel good, to restore psychological balance...you really are worth it.

Professional Help

If you decide to seek professional help, there are certain researched and effective treatments that can help you to work through the traumatic incidents that you have endured.....

Here we mention a few of the best......

Eye Movement DesensitisationReprocessing (EMDR)

Eye Movement Desensitisation Reprocessing (more commonly known as EMDR), is a form of psychotherapy developed in the 1980s by American psychologist Francine Shapiro.

During a stroll in the park, Shapiro made a chance observation that certain eye movements appeared to reduce the negative emotion associated with her own traumatic memories.

When she experimented, she found that others also exhibited a similar response to eye movements, and so she set about conducting controlled studies before developing a multiphase approach to trauma reduction.

Researched and evidenced intervention for multiple traumas to benefit individuals who have been psychologically and/or violently assaulted over a prolonged period. It assists in releasing unprocessed information in the brain, lessening the traumatic impact, distressing images, body memories and intense feelings. It allows the client to be free of the 'trauma fog' that may have taken up so much of their thinking time. If you have experienced a trauma, the memory of your traumatic experience may come hurtling back into your mind like a racing tide, pushing you to re-experience the original incident with the same intensity of feeling - like it is taking place in the present moment. While it isn't possible to erase these memories completely, the process of Eye Movement Desensitisation Reprocessing (EMDR) can lessen the impact and rearrange the storage of such memories, allowing you to recall them with less emotion or distress.

There are eight phases to this trauma treatment as follows:

1. History taking often with a time line, symptoms and units of distress, consideration of whether or not EMDR is the best course of action for you and whether or not you are sufficiently resourced to receive it.

2. Preparation for treatment may include, demonstration with tapping techniques, breathing techniques, answering any questions and generally preparing you for your first session.

3-6. From phase three to approximately six, from your initial time line of traumatic incidents, you can start to choose where you would like to start, you will be asked to answer some questions that relate to the incident, which will require positive and negative answers and different sensory responses will be questioned, you will be completely free to choose the exact incident that you feel comfortable with. The EMDR sessions can be provided with hand movements, or bi lateral stimulation, using a set of tappers or light sensory units. These are divided into sets and after each set, you will be asked for feedback. The whole intervention is based on lowering your SUDS (subjective units of distress) and lessening the impact for you.

3-7. The therapist will manage the time in the session so that you finish with a safe place which allows you to feel calmer before leaving.

3-8. The eighth phase, gives you an opportunity to re-evaluate and to make sure all is going well for you and where you need to work to continue with lessening the impact or if you are able to work on a different issue.

Following EMDR, processing will continue as your brain assimilates and integrates all the information.

This is a positive sign that material is being processed.

Below are examples of what other clients have described between sessions. If this is a road you decide to travel, you may want to make a note of any changes that you experience.

- You may feel exhausted or more tired than usual.
- You may be full of vibrant energy.
- Some people experience physical reactions such as a headache or a cold like symptoms.
- Some people report a mushy type feeling in their head.
- You may feel lighter and have a spring in your step.
- You may get a sense that something has changed, but you are not sure what.
- You may experience a temporary loss of concentration while your mind resettles.
- You may experience a few hollow memories of the session but this will be temporary.
- You may be more emotional or less – it is all part of the processing.
- New forgotten memories may surface and unsettle you for a time.
- Processing will continues after the session and you may experience more details as it does.
- You may experience more intense dreams that you are able to remember

Although this list is by no means complete, the reactions are all a perfectly normal part of EMDR.

Brain spotting (BSP)

A powerful, focused treatment method that works by identifying, processing and releasing core neurophysiological sources of emotional/body pain, trauma, dissociation and a variety of other challenging symptoms.

Brainspotting is a simultaneous form of diagnosis and treatment, enhanced with bio lateral sound, which is deep, direct, and powerful yet focused and containing. This is a relatively new intervention which works on the basis of releasing the body from the traumatic memories it holds via the neurobiological pathway.

It is an excellent and useful tool for working with survivors of trauma because it is non-invasive and the client doesn't necessarily need to speak. This technique allows the body to tell the story and in doing so can release repressed experiences of pent up stagnant and toxic agony.

Brainspotting functions as a neurobiological tool to support the clinical healing relationship. There is no replacement for a mature, nurturing therapeutic presence and the ability to engage another suffering human in a safe and trusting relationship where they feel heard, accepted, and understood.

Brainspotting gives us a tool, within this clinical relationship, to a neurobiological location, focus, process, and to release experiences and symptoms that are typically out of reach of the conscious mind and its cognitive and language capacity.

Brainspotting works with the deep brain and the body through its direct access to the autonomic and limbic systems within the body's central nervous system.

Brainspotting is accordingly a physiological tool/treatment, which has profound psychological, emotional, and physical consequences.

It is theorised that Brainspotting taps into and harnesses the body's innate self-scanning capacity to process and release focused areas (systems), which are in a maladaptive homeostasis (frozen primitive survival modes). This may also explain the ability of Brainspotting to often reduce and eliminate body pain and tension associated with physical conditions.

Visual Kinaesthetic Dissociation Technique (VKD)

This is a specific intervention for traumatic incidents. The rewind technique, also known as the fast phobia cure, evolved from the technique developed by Richard Bandler one of the co-founders of Neuro Linguistic Programming (NLP). He called it the VK dissociation technique (the V stands for visual and the K for kinaesthetic — feelings).

The version recommended by the European Therapy Studies Institute has been refined and streamlined, as a result of its own research into why and how best it works. It is highly useful for individuals who, after exposure to traumatic events, have developed PTSD or lesser forms of the condition which is common in those affected by traumatic incident.

Simply described, the technique works by allowing the traumatised individual, whilst in a safe relaxed state, to reprocess the traumatic memory so that it becomes stored as an 'ordinary', albeit unpleasant, and non- threatening memory rather than one that continually activates a terror response.

This is achieved by enabling the memory to be shifted in the brain from the amygdala to the neocortex. The amygdala's role is to alert us to danger and stimulate the body's 'fight or flight' reaction.

Normally, all initial sensations associated with a threatening experience are passed to the amygdala and formed into a sensory memory, which in turn is passed on to the hippocampus and from there to the neocortex where it is translated into a verbal or narrative memory and stored.

When an event appears life- threatening, however, there can be sudden information overload and the sensory memories stay trapped in the amygdala instead of being passed on to, and made sense of by, the neocortex.

While trapped in the amygdala, the trauma memory has no identifiable meaning. It cannot be described, only re-experienced in some sensory form, such as panic attacks or flashbacks. The rewind technique allows that sensory memory to be converted into narrative, and be put into perspective. It is our sense that trauma is often seen within the mental health profession as a long-term problem, and is perhaps more often misdiagnosed than diagnosed.

Rewind, however, puts a trauma into perspective very neatly.

The treatment takes only a short time; perhaps close to the length of time the incident took to occur — a terrible experience but a tiny part of an entire life.

By relocating the traumatic memory from one part of the brain to another — the place where it was meant to end up in the first place, it re-balances the experience within a person's life.

Most of the people we work with just want to put their experience into proper perspective, not suffer symptoms any more, and get on with their lives.

Rewind is not only powerfully effective in that respect, but side effect free.

Relaxation and/or Mindfulness

Both of these are popular for those working within the field of trauma and usually at the first couple of sessions to teach the client how to ground themselves and be Relaxed.

Only by remaining calm can you even begin to quiet the chaos of a damaged psyche. These could be used alongside other treatments, i.e. the Rewind technique works twice as well if combined with a deep relaxation process, as does Critical Incident Debriefing with individuals.

Mindful relaxation can have a powerful impact on our ability to work towards a longer life, to really feel and see what is before us, awareness of such really is the cornerstone of healing and recovery.

Because the brain is in a hi-jacked state in the aftermath of a traumatic incident, those affected may find it more difficult to break down the fog and to accomplish relaxation.

Sensorimotor Psychotherapy

Those affected often carry the trauma within the very cells and muscular system of their body and it can feel difficult to feel safe again.

Engaging with any therapy that offers a combined processing model of release for both the mind and body is crucial for moving forward.

Sensorimotor Psychotherapy is a therapy developed by Dr Pat Ogden that works somatically (physiological memory) with both the mind and body, so that the traumatic memory can be processed effectively, allowing for lessened impact, thus leaving no residue of the traumatic memory.

The body, for a host of reasons, has been left out of the "talking cure." Psychotherapists who have been trained in models of psychodynamic, psychoanalytic, or cognitive therapeutic approaches are skilled at listening to the language and effect of the client.

They track the clients' associations, fantasies, and signs of psychic conflict, distress, and defences.

Yet while the majority of therapists are trained to notice the appearance and even the movements of the client's body, thoughtful engagement with the client's embodied experience has remained peripheral to traditional therapeutic interventions.

~33~

Guided Visualisation

This is a very powerful tool to assist clients affected by trauma. It allows the client to go back, to revisit, and to make changes in previous situations as well as to create a calmness that they were not able to do anything about at the time.

It's useful to have some music in the background, and if possible, soft blankets available on offer, as many people feel quite exposed when they have their eyes closed. Guided Visualisation allows the choice of time and space in the safety of one's own environment where disturbance can be minimal and relaxation can be attained in order to feel the letting go of many painful memories.

~34~

CID - Critical Incident Debriefing or Psychological Debriefing

This a psychological intervention implemented after a major incident. The aim of Critical Incident Debriefing (CID) is to prevent or limit the onset of Post-Traumatic Stress Disorder (PTSD) ideally; this intervention will take place within two to three days after the incident but can be still be beneficial many years after the event.

Debriefing was originally developed for the benefit of emergency services and military personnel but are now available to benefit the general population where they are exposed to a traumatic incidents, such as domestic violence situations.

The most common model employed by debriefers is the Mitchell and Dyregrove model. This consists of a seven-stage process which people are guided through by the debriefer/s. It can be used on groups of people or with individuals.

Cognitive Behavioural Therapy

Cognitive Behavioural Therapy (CBT) is a psychological treatment for mental health conditions. Treatment usually takes between eight and twenty sessions. It is a combination of cognitive therapy, which can modify or eliminate unwanted thoughts and beliefs, and behavioural therapy, which may help to change behaviour in response to those thoughts.

Cognitive techniques (such as challenging negative thoughts) and behavioural techniques (such as exposure therapy that gradually desensitises phobia and relaxation techniques) are used to relieve symptoms of anxiety and depression by changing thoughts, beliefs and behaviour.

CBT is based on the assumption that most unwanted thinking patterns and emotional and behavioural reactions are learned over a long period of time. The aim is to identify the thinking that is causing unwanted feelings and behaviours and to learn to replace this thinking with more positive thoughts. The therapist does not focus on the events from the past (such as childhood) but focuses on current difficulties at the present time. The therapist will be able to teach new skills and new ways of reacting.

EFT - Emotional Freedom Technique

This is an energy healing technique which is based upon the balance within our mind and body. All living creatures need certain elements to sustain life, without these elements such as food, water, love, company, life will cease and on the way the body will become distressed, physically distorted with a myriad of illness and disease and completely unable to function at any kind of normal level.

EFT is effective in restoring balance which consequentially allows the body and brain to seek further assistance in order to function fully again.

This intervention is known to release symptoms with a pattern of tapping with the fingertips on certain areas of the body which do actually correspond to acupuncture

points on the energy meridians. Where there is an imbalance, there is a corresponding blockage in the flow of energy through the meridian system. Tapping points are as follows:

- Eyebrow
- Side of eye
- Under eye
- Under nose
- Chin
- Collar bone
- Karate chop point on side of hand
- Under arm

The tapping helps to release the blockages that were originally established at the source of the traumatic event. Tapping allows the blockage to be released and balance can be restored. This works by processing the original unprocessed information stored in the body.

~37~

Massage Therapy & Yoga

One of the ways to assist with releasing the psoas muscle is with massage therapy, it can offer a deep sense of peace and relaxation for those who feel strong enough to just let it happen.

Those burdened with the traumatic effects of any kind of life threatening trauma can find it difficult to 'let go' as their parasympathetic nervous system continually raises the danger alarm at touch of any kind.

If the client and massage therapist can build a rapport and enough trust to let the treatment commence then this can be a unique type of intervention.

A primary connector between the torso and the leg, the psoas is also an important muscle which affects posture, helps stabilise the spine, and, if it's out of balance, can be a significant contributor to low back and pelvic pain.

The way that the psoas is used in yoga practice can help keep it healthy, strong, and flexible.

Trauma informed yoga is useful in that the teacher will be appropriately trained and professionally informed and aware about triggers, those who dissociate and become easily emotionally overwhelmed and fully competent to assist with those who may experience flashbacks.

The teacher will always be able to make time for you and will be mindful of the safety aspects surrounding the aftermath of those affected by trauma.

~38~

Bowen Technician & Energy Healing Therapies

As Bowen practitioners, the accuracy and the forgiveness applying the Bowen moves anatomically allow both the practitioner and client to be at optimum calmness, providing an environment to explore exactly how their body is responding to challenges in their life, environment, and work and help to understand their stress patterns which can be reflected in their physiological presentations.

Once we move to understanding and witnessing this in the human form the Bowen work can be more directed and results as stated by the clients themselves, observed. In order for clients entering into any of the therapies mentioned and to start the healing towards processing the trauma that they have endured, they need to be resourced (stable) enough to undergo the intensive and often emotionally turbulent interventions, working towards post traumatic growth.

~39~

Krav Maga

For those who feel they need to learn a self defence strategy that is effective and not combative, there is value in researching a class, enrolling and learning the Krav Maga system which is based on principles and concepts.

The system teaches how to defeat unarmed attackers and to deal with guns and knives. It also teaches how to debilitate attackers no matter how big they are which is an excellent skill to have and gives those affected by a violent predator, an extra chance to get away.

It was developed by the son of a Police Chief Inspector in Bratislava. Most importantly the system can be learned quickly and applied under extreme stress. The system is based on simple and reflexive moves that work when needed.

As a constantly evolving system the effectiveness of all the techniques is constantly tested, evaluated and developed.

Remember........that time really does accelerate healing, as you transcend into acceptance of what cannot be changed and work towards newness.

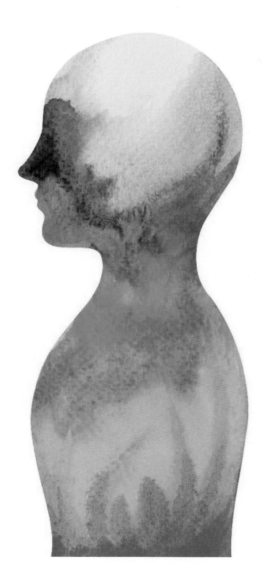

The traumatic incidents must never define who you are. You are a unique amazing and beautiful individual, who has every right to be happy and restored to normal day to day functioning.

A Glimpse of Your Empowered Self

When a person survives any type of traumatic incident, they can often forget who they were before it happened. And what is important is that if you let it, allow it to shine through a NEW and exciting, stronger YOU can emerge from the aftershock.

- Close your eyes and if appropriate you can play some relaxing music in the background, you need feel safe and secure with this exercise.

- Use some breathing techniques such as breathing through your nose into your diaphragm for the count of seven and to breathe out for the count of eleven. Maybe do this three or four times.

- When you are relaxed you can ask a friend to ask you the following leading visualisation.

- Think of your life now, after the trauma has ended.

- Who are you in the here and now today?

- What does that feel like?

- What does that look like?

- Imagine a version of yourself as YOUR new and empowered self.

- Imagine that vision as a clean living well healed version of YOUR true self.

- Look at YOUR new empowered self and see into YOUR heart, asking YOUR dreams and future plans.

- Take a while to allow the image to fill with colour, for rest and relaxation to work its way throughout YOUR entire body.

- So now just imagine walking down a road as YOUR empowered self, towards a fork in the road, if YOU go down the left fork YOU will undoubtedly return to a place where you are not yet ready to start to heal. What does that look like?

- So now, what would it look like if YOU were to go down the right road, the right fork in the road, where YOU are in control of YOUR own decisions, and empowered to the highest that a person can possibly be.

- What does that freedom look like? This free new and empowered self is YOUR next chapter and future!

- So now just continue to make the image of YOUR empowered self as vibrant and strong as YOU possibly can and to hang in to it. YOU can add music to it or imagine carrying out an activity with a new sense of freedom and confidence in the way that YOU can envisage.

- So continue with what YOU have imagined and try to put it into practice and actually start to feel what it might be like to be YOUR empowered self and what life would be like as that free and empowered person.

And a bit more colouring and relaxing – just for you, to indulge yourself in complete self-focus and creation of colours while you do so......

Personal Reflective Journal Notes...

Survival Set of Six

Once you can grasp the 7/11 trauma breathing technique, it can really start to calm your day to day functioning. This allows you to think more clearly and to make positive decisions.

Count of 7 in through the nose   Count of 11 out through the mouth

7/11 Breathing

Breath in through the nose for the count of 7 *(blow up your stomach)*
Breath out through the mouth for the count of 11 *(empty stomach)*
It is the out breath that induces the calm.

Personal Reflective Journal Notes...

Trauma takes its toll on the body as well as the brain. Notice what is happening to your body, it may be responding in many different ways.

If you decide that professional help is what you need, it is important that you find a therapist who is trained and competent to facilitate all areas of processing the traumatic information that is stored in your body.

Although therapists are trained in certain areas of life. Seeing and talking to a complete stranger is not for everyone. If you have someone that you trust enough to talk to and who will listen and nurture you without becoming burdened, allow them in, let them help and support you throughout your recovery process and beyond.

Remember that you are reacting normally to a completely abnormal situation.

Personal Reflective Journal Notes...

When someone has endured a traumatic incident, it can seem like it takes up most of your thinking time.

If you are struggling, you will be able to find a trained therapist to work with you to process what has happened.

We can lose touch very quickly with who we are if we don't engage in activities or choose isolation.

This is about YOU and the strength of the person you are becoming.
Find something that increases your confidence and balance – both in body and mind.

Personal Reflective Journal Notes...

Unfamiliar feelings can be healthy or toxic which can be addressed with a trained professional or even by reading many of the excellent books written on the subject.

PTSD ~ does not define YOU, it is about what has happened to you. You DO have the strength within you to recover.

~53~

The trauma does not need to take over your life, with the right help you really can overcome it.

YOU are a unique and amazing individual, who has every right to be happy and to find a renewed sense of self in normal day to day functioning.

Personal Reflective Journal Notes...

When you feel ready to let it all go, it must be your decision, and you will know when that time has come.

We each have our own pace of how we choose to recover, it takes different time periods for different people. Go at your own pace, always.

Believe in YOU and the power that YOU hold, to recover and to get stronger every day.

We each create our own prisons, of which,
we each hold the key to be released.
Sue J. Daniels

Dissociation

is a powerful and extremely useful part of brain function. It enables an individual (especially children) to effectively 'switch off' their sensory perception and be able to look in on what is or has happened to them as if watching a film, to be recollected later in the same dissociated way.

The brain can assist by dissociating quickly when it feels that what is happening is too much to handle. Reacting like a light switch, it turns off all parts of the event. Dissociation can be a symptom of PTSD (Post Traumatic Stress Disorder) and related disorders.

Can you identify which significant distress triggers manifest as dissociation for you?

COGNITIVE
Words & Phrases:

OLFACTORY - GUSTATORY
Smells & Tastes:

KINAESTHETIC & VISUAL
Feelings and Sensations, People and Places:

OTHER:

Think about how you would prefer to act, feel, think and what your goals are for the future. Traumatic experiences bring to the fore, survival skills which are valuable and useful at the time of the trauma, but which usually become less helpful, and less effective with time.

Sometimes it is possible to become stuck in problem behaviours when pain is not acknowledged, heard, respected, or understood. This is when entering into therapy with a trained therapist for processing the events of the trauma becomes an essential part of recovery and moving forward.

PHYSICAL

Physiological shock
Body still reeling from the traumatic event

Exhaustion – continuous
From lack of sleep

Body Weakness
Fragility

Lowered efficiency of immune system
Due to lack of sleep

Hair Loss – Hair Colour Change
Grey/white in short space of time

Headaches – Aching Eyes
Lack of sleep

Stomach Disturbances
IBS Irritable Bowel Syndrome

Lowered Libido
No interest in intimacy

Sleep Disturbance
Insomnia

Increased Heart Rate
Intermittent Panic Attacks

Hypervigilance
Easily startled,

Loss of balance
Scattered thinking

COGNITIVE

Repeated negative thinking
Self Blaming – bad parent, bad person

Confusion
Chaotic Mind

Distorted thinking patterns
I am going mad

Reduced Self Esteem
No trust in self

Hypervigilance
Easily startled

Temporary loss and/or lack of memory
No head space

Loss of concentration
Academic/work/career/daily routine

Reduced efficiency
Inability to perform on normal level of function

Fear of reprisal
Constant look out for further danger

Loss of pleasure from usual hobbies and activities
Apathy, loss of motivation, lack of interest.

Brain Hijacking
Inability to take in information as trauma has priority

Disbelief
How and why did this happen to me?

EMOTIONAL

Psychosocial difficulties
Social withdrawal, Substance Abuse

Flashbacks
Intrusive & disturbing visual images

Highly & easily distressed and tearful
What might have happened – real or imagined outcomes

Rumination of event & details surrounding it
Inability to stop thinking about the incident and everything involved with it

Hypersensitive in relationships
Fractured Intimate and inter-relationships Self-Harm

Paranoia
Distrust of people, easily offended and unable to relax

Dissociation
Separation of oneself from a person or situation

Terror, hopeless despair
Life will never be the same

Irritability – Bouts of Anger
Not usually displayed

Grief, Pain & Heartache
Often prolonged unaccepted grieving process

Guilt
Self-blame – Survivor Guilt

Rage
Retribution – revenge - self-protection, preservation

Personal Healing & Recovery Plan

(Name _____)

Foreword

YOUR thoughts of the last ten years - bullet pointed list of significant events.

Aims

One to five years ahead of what you want and need to achieve to make your life better for you.

1.

2.

3.

4.

5.

Full Plan

Full plan for the next ten years is..................realistic dreams that you can make become actual facts.

Stakeholders of my future plans & goals:

Family, spouse, children, work, training with who and what I choose to invest in...

~67~

Personal Reflective Journal Notes...

Most Important Priorities for me....

1.

2.

3.

4.

5.

6.

7.

8.

9.

10.

Give yourself time to heal.....to take time for yourself...

Traumatic incidents, whether they are criminal, workplace, within our working remit or in whichever way that they present are what happens to us ~ not we have created.

Anger

Anger is often underpinned by pain and frustration, at what happened, at those who hurt you, and possibly the fact that you are unable to talk about it with loved ones, for fear of upsetting them. Sometimes anger can be called; the backbone of healing – a powerful and freeing force,

There are positive ways to channel this anger, physical activity, talking to someone you trust or a trained counsellor or trauma focused therapist. You can write a journal of your experience to alleviate the way you feel and transform those feelings into a healthier emotion.

Disbelief and shock – in the beginning it may have been hard to come to terms with what has happened and life may seem chaotic, you may go over and over scenes in your mind unable to shut it out.

These thoughts may take up one hundred per cent of your thinking time, leaving no space for anything else in your life. This can be distressing and disturbing to the balance of the mind. It is important to know that this will not last forever and it really is possible to put the pieces of your life back together and to move on.

Release is beautiful, find a way to let it go. Find a way to restore your life for you, to the joy it really can be.

Seek, keep searching and you will find the right way to heal for you.

Healing is not about people feeling sorry for you, which is why talking to friends or family does not always help. Healing is about regaining the power and control that has temporarily been taken away from you.

Healing and restoration of YOU...

There are excellent researched, proven techniques and interventions available for those who have suffered traumatic events and to enable lessening of the impact – it really does not have to ruin your life.

YOUR investment in YOU....

It really is important for you to know that it is completely possible to get through this and move on, you can assist your natural ability to heal both emotionally and physically.

The pain can be likened to s deepening barbed splinter and the more the innocent survivor tries to ignore it, the sharper the barbs become and the deeper the splinter goes, taking with it, searing emotional pain. With the right help, it IS possible to remove that splinter.

A New Growth

Visit a garden centre or plant nursery. Purchase your favourite tree, bush or whatever suits you and plant it somewhere significant to you – let it represent the **new you**, the **stronger you**. Watch it grow and get stronger each year.

Personal Reflective Journal Notes...

Try colouring in this little beauty......

"Today I choose life. Every morning when I wake up I can choose joy,
happiness, negativity, pain... To feel the freedom that comes from being able
to continue to make mistakes and choices - today I choose to feel life, not to
deny my humanity but embrace it".
Kevyn Aucoin

Sometimes you may need to find a way to ground yourself when you are feeling less than confident, panicky ...try the following grounding techniques.

- Using the 7/11 breathing technique, breathe in a colour that makes you feel calm and in control.

- Breathe out the colour that has the strongest association with the panic and fear.

- Enjoy a further 15 – 30 minute breathing exercise.

- Think about your Empowered Self grounding his/her self, right now.

- Listen to calming music/meditation.

- Go for a brisk walk.

- Power nap.

- Plan your weekend.

- Enjoy a nourishing meal or snack.

- Telephone or text to family or friends.

- Complete an exercise in this work book.

- Do the crossword/word search

If it helps, make some notes under the options about the techniques that help you the most.....

Guilt can be healthy or toxic, which may be addressed with a trained professional or even by reading many of the excellent books written on the subject.

Guilt ~ The purpose of guilt can evoke further feelings and helps us to consider how or if we could have acted differently.

Survivor Guilt

After surviving a traumatic incident, it can create a profound sense of guilt. People may have died. Not everyone will experience this type of feeling but it is a completely understandable and normal reaction. The knowledge that someone has died and you have survived.

Write down 10 reasons that you think may be how you experience survivor guilt?

1.

2.

3.

4.

5.

6.

7.

8.

9.

10.

Crossword Time

Across:

1. Ready for action
3. Group of musicians
5. Not here
6. Less coloured
8. Similar to
11. Body of gardening enthusiasts
12. Take one at a time
15. Felines
16. Larger than life
17. Water from the eye
18. Highest

Down:

1. To experience an emotion
2. To speak with another
3. To go around
4. To recolour clothing perhaps
9. Concept
10. Tool for rubbing out
13. Diplomacy
14. To hold up
15. Baby bed

Trauma Stress Questionnaire Workplace related stress...

Circle a number from 1 to 5 that is most appropriate to you.

1 = Lowest 2 = Highest

a) In the last month how often have you been upset by another person's behaviour at work or at home or both?

1   2   3   4   5

b) In the last month, how often have you felt that you were unable to control the important things in your life?

1   2   3   4   5

c) In the last month, have you felt nervous, stressed or anxious to the point where you have needed relaxants (sleep medication) prescribed medication?

1   2   3   4   5

d) In the last month, how often have you felt that demands were piling up so high that you could not overcome or find a solution?

1   2   3   4   5

e) In the last month, have you felt pointlessness to life in general?

1   2   3   4   5

f) In the last month, have you felt disillusioned at work, at home or both?

1   2   3   4   5

g) In the last month have you felt trapped, claustrophobic emotionally, physically or financially?

1   2   3   4   5

h) In the last month, would you say you have spent much time doing activities i.e. sport relaxation that YOU particularly like?

1   2   3   4   5

i) Do you have any current physical issues especially, skin complaints, excessive pain or continuous cold and flu like symptoms?

1   2   3   4   5

j) Have you experienced a trauma in your life where you thought that your life or the lives of others was threatened with death

1   2   3   4   5

k) Do you have a general sleep pattern of undisturbed peace for six or more hours per night?

1   2   3   4   5

l) Do you use alcohol or other chemicals as a way to relax, forget or detach from reality?

1   2   3   4   5

m) Do you get angry or irritable easily either at home or at work or both?

1   2   3   4   5

n) Do you regularly drink coffee, cocoa cola or other stimulants daily?

1   2   3   4   5

o) Would you say that generally you feel tired a lot of the time?

1   2   3   4   5

p) Do you ever feel like you have given so much that you have nothing left to give?

1   2   3   4   5

q) Do you find yourself ever bursting into tears or becoming distressed for no apparent reason but a hundred reasons all in one?

1   2   3   4   5

r) Would you say that you work or engage with life at 100 miles per hour most of the time?

1   2   3   4   5

s) Do you ever wake up with a feeling of dread, psychologically unable to move your legs and body because it just all feels too heavy?

| 1 | 2 | 3 | 4 | 5 |

t) Do you regularly take work home with you at night?

| 1 | 2 | 3 | 4 | 5 |

u) Are you able to find a work/life/home balance and engage with interpersonal relationship without thinking about the trauma?

| 1 | 2 | 3 | 4 | 5 |

v) Do you ever feel overwhelmed by people seemingly not acknowledging what you do or say, or what you have been through

| 1 | 2 | 3 | 4 | 5 |

w) Do you ever feel temporary detached from reality with nothing making much sense?

| 1 | 2 | 3 | 4 | 5 |

x) Would you say that your use of alcohol, prescription drugs or other stimulants has increased in the last three months?

| 1 | 2 | 3 | 4 | 5 |

Stress Questionnaire Results

{24 – 48}

Stress level is indicated as low and individual has managed to maintain a strong work/life balance. Very few signs shown of any stress, no trauma residue and manages stress related situations well in general terms.

{48 – 72}

Stress level is indicated as moderate. Individual shows some signs of stress, there are signs of a tendency for associated symptoms and losing sight of work/life/joy balance. Generally copes well with stress.

{72 – 96}

Stress level is indicated as high. Individual shows many signs of stress and hyperactivity (body unable to calm down) it is likely that individual is struggling with issues and or unable to delegate efficiently resulting in possible overload leading to a burn out situation. There may be underlying issues or unfinished business in the client's life whether historic or present.

{96 – 120}

Stress level indication is extremely high and the individual shows severe signs of the dangers of emotional, physical and mental exhaustion, PTSD and/or associated symptoms which have been brought on by excessive and prolonged stress, traumatic incident/s that have been previously left unaddressed.

Notes...Remember YOU! Remember the activities that you used to enjoy.

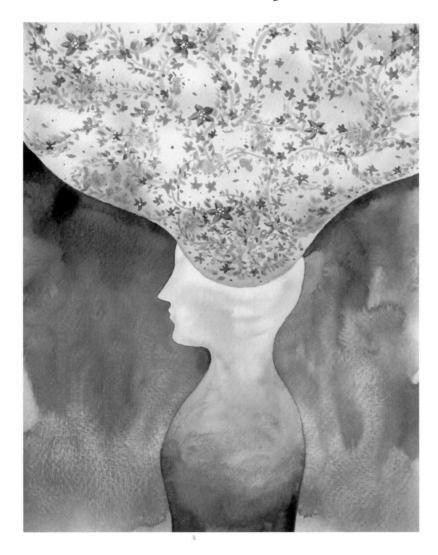

Try to reintroduce them into your life or find new ones.

Trauma Tapestry: A Seven-Step Process

1. This is a great exercise if you enjoy or are good at drawing – let us explain how the trauma tapestry works from beginning to end. This is not a quick fix and there is no time limit.

2. So, can you start to draw images of the traumatic incident, from your own perspective. They don't have to be pieces of art, stick drawings will be absolutely fine, as long as they come from your own memories, thoughts and feelings.

3. When you have drawn two or three pictures and you are happy with what they mean to you, you can start to join the pictures together with tape in exactly the order that feels right for you.

4. If you are happy to continue with the drawings – keep going so that you can explore the reasons for choosing certain colours.

5. Keep the pictures going until you've drawn everything that you feel is enough. As you start to tape the pictures together you will create the beginnings of your unique tapestry.

6. When you feel that it is finished, it is time to find a safe place to set light to it. Suggestions might be to burn it in a metal bin or an incinerator. It is crucial that you save all of the ashes.

7. And now it is time to decide what you will do with the ashes – here are some examples.
   - Put ashes into a pot or into the earth and grow a plant so that something beautiful comes from something not so beautiful.
   - Put ashes into a piece of muslin and tie to an air balloon and let it go, watch until it disappears out of sight.
   - Take the ashes in a box or an envelope to a significant place or the where the attack/s happened and leave or scatter them there.
   - Put ashes in the toilet, skip, rubbish dump anywhere that is significant.
   - Release ashes into a river or stream (making sure there is no plastic contained within).

Now that you are coming to the end of the workbook

List ten ways that you have found to help yourself recover, that might be making an appointment to see a counsellor or support worker, it might be taking up a new activity that releases somatic (body memory) trauma. Or anything in fact that YOU believe has helped you along your pathway to recovery.

1.

2.

3.

4.

5.

6.

7.

8.

9.

10.

Healing and keeping emotionally safe....

Above all, don't let anyone rush you, take your time, this is your journey, no one else's. Remember that you have been acting normally to a completely abnormal situation.

All recovery needs to be at a pace that suits you.

"And once the storm is over, you won't remember how you made it through, how you managed to survive.

You won't even be sure whether the storm is really over.

But one thing is certain...

When you come out of the storm, you won't be the same person who walked in.

That's what this storm is all about".

Haruki Murakami ~ Kafka on the Shore
ISBN 1-84343-110-6

Other resources in this category, available to order from Amazon Online and all major High Street Bookshops.

#Me Time – Therapeutic Workbook for those affected by Rape and Sexual Violence

#Me Time = ISBN 978-0-9932289-8-8

****

L.A.V.A. – Therapeutic Workbook for those affected by Domestic Violence and Abuse

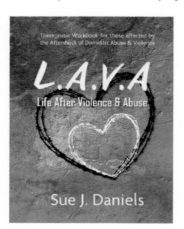

L.A.V.A. – ISBN 978-1-9160933-0-0

****

Working with the Aftershock of Domestic Violence and Abuse
(Available in Paperback and E-Book Format)

Paperback ISBN - 978-0-9932289-9-5

E-Book ISBN - B07KDXCZQY

****

Working with the Trauma of Rape and Sexual Violence
(Available in Paperback and E-Book Format)

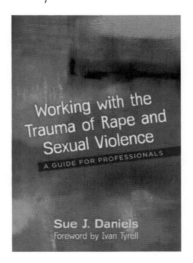

Paperback ISBN - 978-0-9927848-9-8

E-Book ISBN - B01M7NO4OX

****

Men's Little Book of Solace – Pocket Self Help Book

Men's Little Book of Solace ~ ISBN ~ 978-0-9927848-1-2

Men's Little Book of Solace ~ ISBN ~ 978-0-9927848-1-2

****

Pocket Book of Power – Pocket Self Help Book

Pocket Book of Power ~. ISBN = 978-0-9932289-9-5

Pocket Book of Power ~. ISBN = 978-0-9932289-9-5

****

Crossword Answers

Across:

1. Fit
3. Band
5. Away
6. Pale
8. Like
11. R.H.S
12. Step
15. Cats
16. Epic
17. Tear
18. Top

Down:

1. Feel
2. Talk
3. Bypass
4. Dye
9. Idea
10. Eraser
13. Tact
14. Prop
15. Cot

References

Griffin, J and Tyrrell, I (2001*). The Shackled Brain: how to release locked-in patterns of trauma.* HG Publishing, East Sussex.

Griffin, J Tyrrell, I (2006) *Human Givens Joe Griffin & Ivan Tyrell* (HG Publishing)

Van der Kolk BA, *The compulsion to repeat the trauma: re-enactment, re-victimisation, and masochism.* Psychiatr Clin North Am 1989; 12(2):389-411.

Daniels, Sue J, (2011) *Quote - We each make our own prison.*

Hamilton K. Laurell. Mistral's Kiss: *Urban Fantasy – (Merry Gentry 5)* Bantam Press (4 Dec. 2006)

Aucoin, Kevyn. *Face Forward:* Publisher: Little, Brown & Company; New Ed edition (31 Oct. 2001)

Stoddard, Alexandra. Alexandra Brandon Stoddard, born circa 1967 *is an associate editor of The Hill is a regular contributor to The Hill's Pundits Blog and a regular guest giving political commentary on MSNBC, FOX News, CNN, PBS, HBO, BBC and Court TV - http://www.alexandrastoddard.com/meet.asp*

Murakami, Haruki. Kafka on the Shore: *Kafka Tamura runs away from home at fifteen, under the shadow of his father's dark prophecy.* Publisher: Vintage. New Ed edition (6 Oct. 2005)